RIDE YOUR ELEVATOR PITCH TO THE PENTHOUSE!
INTRODUCE YOURSELF TO OPPORTUNITY

DAVE BRICKER

RIDE YOUR ELEVATOR PITCH TO THE PENTHOUSE!

INTRODUCE YOURSELF TO OPPORTUNITY

He who tooteth not his own horn,
yay the same shalt not get tooted

—John Strider Nation

with gratitude to
Will Ezell and Bruce Turkel

Introduction

You're attending yet another networking meeting where participants are asked to present round-the-room introductions. As each guest steps up to speak, time slows down. The seconds ooze by like honey across a glacier as each attendee rambles on about what they do, how long they've been doing it, who they've done it for and … sorry … where was I?

The positioning statement or "elevator pitch" — named after an imagined scenario in which we meet someone in an elevator and have a short time to introduce ourselves before one of us reaches our desired floor — is an essential professional tool — a tool that must be kept razor sharp and as ready to deploy as a handshake and a smile — and yet, most professionals are woefully bad at introducing themselves.

How can we share a compelling authentic value story before our elevator pitch winds up in the basement? We've got 30 seconds at best … and that's only if our opening line attracts enough attention to keep our listeners engaged for more than five. A ten- or fifteen-second introduction is better than a 30-second mini-biography.

Given its importance, demonstrating the ability to deliver a compelling elevator pitch should be a prerequisite for high school graduation. Instead, most professionals struggle to communicate their value to the people who need them.

If we can't communicate our value—what we have to offer—to the people who need it, we probably won't get hired to solve their problems.

And that's a problem of its own!

Why is it that so many of us find it easy to explain what we *do* but when it comes to explaining *why* someone should work with us, we're tongue-tied.

How can you ride a good elevator pitch all the way to the penthouse? This guide will show you how.

A Storytelling Approach

Stories — in books, movies, articles, ad campaigns — are the most powerful form of communication we have.

Stories are *sticky*. Sometimes we finish *really lame* books and movies because we have to find out how they end. Maybe you have a favorite movie you've watched over and over and over. And there must be a reason your kid can watch *Sleeping Beauty* 614 times!

Stories attract and hold our attention. So doesn't it make sense that the power of story will help us create an elevator pitch that attracts and holds the attention of the right people in the room?

What's Different About *Business* Storytelling?

Popular storytelling strategies like Joseph Campbell's "hero's journey" work well for epic films and books, but these narratives deal with *themes* like good and evil.

A Hero's Journey

In George Lucas's *Star Wars,* Luke Skywalker buys two droids as part of a routine work day. When one of them runs away, he tracks it into the desert where he's ambushed by the Sand People. After he's rescued by Obi Wan Kenobi, the lost droid shows him Princess Leia's message. Luke returns home to find his home in ruins, and that those routine work days are a thing of the past. He's off to discover The Force and battle evil Darth Vader with Obi Wan as his guide.

Every component of the Star Wars story is a classic "Hero's Journey." Screenwriters literally have this formula broken down to what page of the script to introduce a particular piece of the journey on!

As professionals looking for new business, our goal is not to keep a theater full of moviegoers entertained for two hours. We want to share simple, concise stories that persuade — simple, concise, and persuasive being three hallmarks of a good business story. To accomplish our goals, we'll dispense with the complexity and apply a storytelling model that's appropriately simple and concise.

StorySailing:® A Simple Structure for Business Storytelling

When I was a young man, I was introduced to a group of voyagers who lived aboard their small sailboats in Miami's free anchorage. They didn't have much money and their boats were humble but they sailed the world on a whim. Their stories enthralled me.

The idea that you could have real life adventures without cracking open a book or a buying a ticket to the movies had never occurred to me.

By the time I graduated college I was living aboard my own small sailboat. Six months later, I left for the

Bahamas with $30 and a locker full of food and dreams to find stories of my own—and over many thousands of miles I accomplished just that.

Perhaps you sense a hero's journey coming on, but you can read that story in a different book.[1] My fascination with sailing and story led me to explore what a story is (and isn't), how it works, and why it captures our attention like nothing else. That led me to discover StorySailing®—a simple story structure that works for pretty much any message you'd care to create. It consists of one golden rule and four simple elements.

The Golden Rule of Storytelling

Stories are always about people. It could be about *metaphorical* people—like aliens or talking animals—but **a story is always about people.**

---

1 Bricker, Dave. *The Blue Monk: A Memoir.* Essential Absurdities Press, 2014.

It's simple. If we're talking about prices, processes, ingredients, functions, features, or data, we're not talking about people.

Not talking about people = not telling stories.

Not telling stories = not connecting.

Not connecting = not selling.

We can do better.

A Note on Selling

If you find the S-word (selling) offensive, rethink the idea that selling has anything to do with asking people for money.

We sell our ideas, credibility, suitability, and trustworthiness every day.

Anyone who's asked for a date, applied for a job, tried to put a child to bed, or struggled to entice the family dog to step into the bathtub is selling.

We're all selling every day!

> And all those sad little people who skip the selling process and try to jump directly to the transaction haven't figured out that begging never helped a relationship. Their tacky and ineffective positioning statements might sound something like:
>
> *I'm in the _____ business. Pay me!*

Open a recent uninvited email promotion or look at an advertisement in a printed magazine. Billions of dollars are wasted on ineffective messages every year. These clumsy communiqués fail because they're not about people.

We hear about the secret ingredient, the five-step process, the square footage, the horsepower, and the longer battery life, but we don't hear much about *us*.

One of the first lessons you'll learn in Marketing 101 is:

Sell the benefits, not the features.

That's because benefits, not features, are connected to *people*.

If our pitches are about what we do rather than about who we do it for, the magic disappears.

Doctor Franklin is a dentist.

We can guess he works on molars, incisors, and bicuspids. He performs implant and root canal procedures—like every other dentist.

Yawn!

Thanks but I already have a dentist I like.

But if Dr. Franklin is a "smile architect" who makes his patients "confident and kissable," it just might be my existing dentist who ends up being "just another dentist."

What they *do* is the same but what they *offer* is something entirely different.

See how a boring factoid—"I'm a dentist"—can be transformed into a captivating story about the patients he helps—a story about *people?* If you have discolored or crooked or missing teeth, Dr. Franklin's story about lost confidence could be relevant to *you*. And that's how connections are made.

StorySailing: Every Story Begins with an Authentic Conflict

We don't introduce ourselves at business meetings and networking events to make friends. We want to connect with the right people so we can pursue *business opportunities*. We want to meet people who struggle with problems we can solve.

That sounds simple enough: Anyone who has a problem wants a solution.

But how many times have you had a friend, colleague, or family member ask you to listen to them explain their problem? And how often is it that it dawns on you a few minutes into their exposition: *I don't think what you're complaining about is really your problem!?*

Other people's problems are too easy to see. Our own problems are a different matter. We ignore red flags, wait too long to pull the plug, blame others for our misfortunes, and do whatever we can to forestall the conclusion that much of our pain and woe is of our own making.

When creating a business story, we must identify the **authentic conflict.** If we choose an inauthentic conflict, we end up with an ineffective message.

Dudley is offered a new Porsche 911 Turbo for his sixteenth birthday. His father tells him he can choose red or black but not yellow, and this makes him very upset.

Poor Dudley! Boo-hoo! What an entitled little snot! Dudley's story doesn't appeal to us because we've all got *much* more serious problems to deal with! His story doesn't touch on any conflict we can identify with. We don't care.

So what *does* make us care?

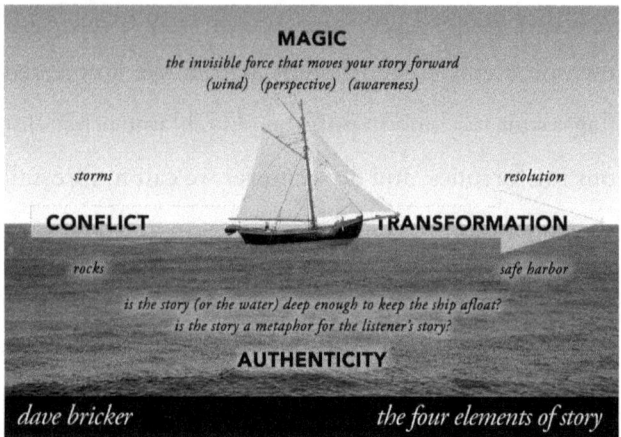

dave bricker   *the four elements of story*

An authentic message addresses a survival-level need. We are all biologically programmed to care about:

1. **Food**—We all have to eat to survive.
2. **Love**—We all want to be cared for, respected, listened to, valued, and understood.
3. **Shelter**—We all need shelter—a place to live.
4. **Sex**—We are all programmed to make new people, even if we elect not to.
5. **Status**—Higher status in the tribe increases our odds of finding love and making new people.

6. **Safety**—We all want to not get hurt or killed.
7. **Family**—We care for and protect our loved ones (and those who fail at that are usually driven to do so by unmet needs higher up this list).

Yes, we all want more money, but a persuasive message connects to the authentic needs we'll meet when we *spend* the money. Perhaps we'll buy food, acquire a new home, buy school books for our children, or purchase new clothes that make us feel attractive so we can find a job or a mate. We can't eat money!

You've heard this one before: People buy with emotion and then justify their purchases with logic.

Remember our dentist, Dr. Franklin? He offers to help people who have lost confidence because of the condition of their teeth. If they're not "confident and kissable," they're going to miss out on opportunities that are more than just business-related. If they can't smile, they can't connect with *anybody*. *Intellectually,* his patients know that any dentist could perform the necessary procedures to straighten, whiten, or replace their unhealthy teeth, but *emotionally,* they want someone who connects with their authentic problem.

Authentic Conflict Leads to Authentic Transformation

Bernice wants her missing tooth replaced because she wants to look attractive in the mirror … and to a potential life partner. In the story she finds love. Maybe our listener will, too. *Transformation!*

Juan knows that fresh breath and a winning smile will help him succeed at his sales job. Earning the trust and respect of prospects will enable him to eat and pay for his house. In the story, he closes a big deal he would have lost before because of his poor oral health. *Transformation!*

As a physician, Dr. Cooper relies on his dentist to help him convey the highest standards of self-care and hygiene. Otherwise, he'll fail to earn the trust and respect of his own patients. His status as a professional caretaker is a core part of his practice. In the story, a new patient leaves because Dr. Cooper's teeth don't suggest that he takes care of himself. *How will he take care of me?* thinks the patient. But after a few visits to Dr. Franklin, Dr. Cooper's credibility is restored. *Transformation!*

Though the services we provide may be practical—like getting a drain unclogged or a power steering pump replaced—the *meaningful transformation*—the *authentic transformation*—we deliver has to do with survival-level needs. When we create our elevator pitch, we'll think about what our ideal prospect's journey is from authentic conflict to authentic transformation.

Target the Right Prospects. Kick ASK!

Let's say we're introducing ourselves to 40 people in a room at a networking event. If all of them say, "Yes!"

we'll find ourselves overrun with new business. Usually, a small room contains only a few of our ideal prospects. So instead of marketing to *everyone,* our goal is to create a message that appeals to the authentic needs of our ideal clients.

So here's the first part of your elevator pitch:

The easiest way to target your ideal prospects is to *ask them* to identify with the authentic conflict you provide transformation for. Reference the problem you solve (and remember to pause after you ask a question so your listener has time to think about its relevance to them).

Do *you* struggle with _____?

Did *you* ever wish you could _____?

Do *you* want to _____?

Is _____ costing *you* (<u>time</u> /<u>stress</u> / <u>money</u>)?

If you work with a particular type of client, bundle your specialization information with the above.

Are you a small business owner who struggles with _____?

Did you ever wish you could _____ in your consulting practice?

Do you want to find more (<u>coaching</u> / <u>editing</u> / <u>executive</u>) clients?

Are you a manufacturer who's losing (<u>time</u> / <u>stress</u> / <u>money</u>) to _____?

Don't worry about the demographics of your ideal client. As a professional who trades in results, connect with people who identify with the conflict you just shared. Create a net with a wide enough weave to allow the little fish to pass through.

Get Rid of Your I-Infection!

So many people love to talk about themselves.

"I do this and I do that."

"I work with Fortune 100 companies like MegaCorp."

"I help contractors save time and money."

"I find leads for coaches."

Ladies, have you ever been out on a first date with that guy? The minutes slog by as you wait for your girlfriend to rescue you with the phony emergency call. The second date never happens.

Vote yourself off the I-land!

Stories are always about people so begin with "you"—not *you* you—*them* you.

Agitate the Problem

When we're in conflict, nothing is more annoying than unsolicited advice. Rather than foisting our solutions on our prospects, we want to encourage them to take action. Even when we're *asked* for advice, wise questions are more powerful than smart answers. After we ask our conflict-identifying questions, we want our prospect to decide to seek a solution on their own. When they feel pressured or criticized, most people let their problems simmer. When we artfully agitate the problem, we encourage our listener to take action — not because *we* want them to but because *they* realize they need to.

What will your business look like a year from now if you don't do something about it?

Are you going to keep allowing competitors to walk away with your best clients?

How much longer will you stay in business if no one can find you?

Wouldn't you rather spend all those overtime hours with your loved ones?

Agitate the Problem, Not the Person!

Trading on peoples' insecurities is a deplorable way to do business. Positioning yourself as anyone's last hope is a narcissistic power play. Avoid toxic, quasi-motivational messages like:

If you're not willing to invest in yourself, you're just not serious about success. Failure is free. You can have as much as you want.

Only 5% of the people who try succeed in this business. Do you have the discipline to beat those odds? If not, there's the door.

If you're not ready now, that's okay. Just keep doing it the wrong way and come back when you're tired and hungry and frustrated enough to do it the right way.

Offer *Transformation*

Don't burden your elevator pitch with the name of your program or formula or method. You can explain *how* you work after you've successfully inspired a conversation. Use an imperative verb[2] to start a call to action that references a meaningful outcome. Use "heart words" as much as possible. Verbs like "use," "put," "develop," and "is," are correct and functional but they're *boring;* they don't deliver much emotional, inspirational, or aspirational impact.

Heart Words

Create	Reveal	Discover	Master
Explore	Ignite	Reinvent	Transcend
Conquer	Succeed	Grow	Future-proof
Build	Crush	Surpass	Detonate
Finish	Inspire	Aspire	Triumph

---

2 Imperative verbs are commands. *Discover* this. *Reveal* the truth.

Master the secrets to _____.

Discover the strategies used by
successful _____.

Explore the techniques used by the world's
best_____.

Or try a bit of rhyme or alliteration, even if the verbs aren't especially heartfelt.

Put your plumbing problems in the past.

Want fewer hours for higher pay?
Hire a guide to point the way.

Share Your Name and a Catchy Title

Here's some commonsense advice you'll rarely hear:
If you state your name at the beginning of your

Stink Words

I had the opportunity to study with a successful copywriter. He was quick to tell me, "Dave, not everyone thinks the way you do!"

I love to learn, but sadly, many people associate *learning* with uninspiring teachers, arcane textbooks, and boring classes. "Learn," he declared, "is a stink word!"

"Work" is another stink word.

"Need" is another.

Not everyone thinks the way you do! In your elevator pitch, avoid telling people what they'll learn, who you work with, or what they need.

introduction, people will forget it *instantly*. Nobody cares who's talking until they care about what's being said. Inspire interest in solving a problem first using the techniques introduced earlier; *then* introduce yourself as a solution.

I'm Juan, your (expert, guru, guide, etc.).

I'm Bert and I help (type of client) with (type of transformation).

Close with a reason to contact you and a call to action. What should they do when they're ready to say, "yes?"

When you want to (grow your business, find more clients, keep your employees engaged), let's talk.

When you're tired of (losing time / stress / money), connect with me at my-website.com.

When you're ready to start (making money, growing your influence, finding better clients), let's connect.

Start your path to prosperity by connecting with me on LinkedIn.

Own Your Zone!

If you're having difficulty figuring out what your zone of genius is, ask the people who know you well. It may be that you do something remarkable but you don't think much of it because it's always been easy for you. If you fix stuff that's broken, have a way with words, or love to draw, you may not think of those gifts as anything special.

When your friends call you "brilliant" or compliment you for being a "wizard," they may be right! Own your zone of genius. Stay humble about it but own it.

What Makes You Different?

We discussed **conflict, transformation,** and **authenticity.** The fourth and final element of storytelling is **magic**—a powerful, invisible force—the wind that moves our metaphorical ship of story from the stormy seas of conflict, across the deep waters of authenticity, and into the safe port of transformation. Your zone of genius might be your talent. It could be your insight, your experience, your team, your specialized equipment, your professional values, techniques you've invented, or any number of other qualities that make you *you*. Just being punctual will distinguish you from 95% of your competitors! Narrow it down from there.

If you're a realtor or a financial manager or a dentist or a plumber, what you *do* is pretty much the same thing your competitors do. Differentiate yourself by being likable, empathetic, and fun. Punch up your elevator pitch and make it memorable by adding an element of clever rhyme or alliteration.

Pitch Time

The following examples don't adhere strictly to the recipe above but the essential elements are there.

Rules are made to be broken. Don't sacrifice a creative opportunity on the altar of formulaic thinking.

The sample pitches below present two versions, a long one and a short one. The full version is best for round-the-room introductions. If time is short use the final lines (underlined) to create a super-quick intro. When greeting someone face-to-face, the shorter version sounds less commercial — more like something you'd say to an individual and less like a presentation you'd give to a room full of prospects.

Are you an entrepreneur who struggles to maintain a steady flow of qualified customers? What's the point of building anything without a success plan? <u>Discover the strategies that turn small businesses into *big* businesses. I'm Sharon, your strategic growth consultant. Call me when you're ready to make a profit</u>.

Are you losing opportunities to boring sales pitches and wasting time at boring meetings? Master the secrets of top professional speakers and champion sales leaders. <u>Engage your colleagues and prospects and motivate people to say "Yes!" I'm Tom from Stagecrafters. Ask me about presentation skills programs that mean business</u>.

Are your spreadsheets thousands of rows of pure confusion? How much time, stress, and money would you save with a simple and intuitive way to manage income and expenses? <u>I'm Martha and I turn Excel into *excellent* results. When you're ready to take control of your numbers, ask me about a free consultation today</u>.

For years, you've tried to write that book, but you run into dead ends, lose focus, or just transform the jumble of ideas in your head into a jumble of ideas on your screen. Stop staring at the keyboard and get the support serious authors depend on. <u>I'm Michael the book sherpa and I help visionary people organize, write, and publish visionary books. Call me when you're ready to turn pages into wages</u>.

What should you post on YouTube, FaceBook, Instagram, TikTok, and LinkedIn and how often? What about blog posts and podcasts? How can you build meaningful business connections when you have to manage all that media? <u>I'm Lindsay, the *postess* with the mostest. Send me a private message when you're ready to put social media to work for you instead of the other way around</u>.

When it's your turn to speak up do you know what to say and how to say it? Do your words enrage … or do your words engage? Do your words deflect or do your words connect? <u>Turn that mess into a message! I'm Dave Bricker, business</u>

storytelling expert. If you want to say it, share it, or sell it, bring me your story; I'll help you tell it.

The simple elevator pitch carries a great deal of weight. The first time I tried mine out, I was *astonished*. After my introduction, the room went silent for a moment and then burst into applause. That wasn't my goal (and a colleague teased me later over just how unprepared I had been to receive that level of attention). Nevertheless, as a self-professed "business storytelling expert," my short, powerful introduction offers me an opportunity to show instead of tell.

Give your elevator pitch the attention it deserves. Your listeners will do the same for you. And you just might find yourself getting off at the penthouse!

Create Your Elevator Pitch

1 | **Identify the authentic conflict**
What's the *real* problem?

2 | **Clarify the transformation**
Forget about what you *do*. What results do you deliver?

3 | **Do you cater to a specific audience?**
Do you help "professionals" in general or do
you work with contractors or realtors?

4 | **Kick ASK!**
Ask who has the authentic problem you solve

5 | **Agitate the Problem**
Ask what will happen if they don't take action.
Inspire them to hold themselves accountable

6 | **Share your name and a catchy title**
Attach your name to a provocative description

7 | **Call to Action**
Tell them what the next step is. How can they engage?

For engaging business communications programs
and smart storytelling strategies, visit:

https://storysailing.com